You're NOT a Monkey!

By Christina H. McKeon

YOU'RE NOT A MONKEY!

Copyright © 2020 Christina H. McKeon

1405 SW 6th Avenue • Ocala, Florida 34471 • Phone 352-622-1825 • Fax 352-622-1875
Website: www.atlantic-pub.com • Email: sales@atlantic-pub.com
SAN Number: 268-1250

No part of this publication may be reproduced, stored in a retrieval system, or transmitted in any form or by any means, electronic, mechanical, photocopying, recording, scanning, or otherwise, except as permitted under Section 107 or 108 of the 1976 United States Copyright Act, without the prior written permission of the Publisher. Requests to the Publisher for permission should be sent to Atlantic Publishing Group, Inc., 1405 SW 6th Avenue, Ocala, Florida 34471.

Library of Congress Control Number: 2020905818

LIMIT OF LIABILITY/DISCLAIMER OF WARRANTY: The publisher and the author make no representations or warranties with respect to the accuracy or completeness of the contents of this work and specifically disclaim all warranties, including without limitation warranties of fitness for a particular purpose. No warranty may be created or extended by sales or promotional materials. The advice and strategies contained herein may not be suitable for every situation. This work is sold with the understanding that the publisher is not engaged in rendering legal, accounting, or other professional services. If professional assistance is required, the services of a competent professional should be sought. Neither the publisher nor the author shall be liable for damages arising herefrom. The fact that an organization or website is referred to in this work as a citation and/or a potential source of further information does not mean that the author or the publisher endorses the information the organization or website may provide or recommendations it may make. Further, readers should be aware that Internet websites listed in this work may have changed or disappeared between when this work was written and when it is read.

TRADEMARK DISCLAIMER: All trademarks, trade names, or logos mentioned or used are the property of their respective owners and are used only to directly describe the products being provided. Every effort has been made to properly capitalize, punctuate, identify, and attribute trademarks and trade names to their respective owners, including the use of ® and ™ wherever possible and practical. Atlantic Publishing Group, Inc. is not a partner, affiliate, or licensee with the holders of said trademarks.

Printed in the United States

PROJECT MANAGER: Kassandra White

This book is dedicated to my daughter Charlotte, whom I love to the moon and back and will forever be my sunshine.

—Mommy

At times, when we are young we may feel choiceless. Yet, in fact we all have the choice to be kind.

Charlotte was one of those young girls who chose to be kind to EVERYBODY, even if they were unkind to her!

She was a 2nd grader with blond hair, glasses, and a big heart.

One day at school the bell rang. "All right children," their teacher, Miss Luna, said kindly, "please, place your reading books in your desks neatly. Then you may quietly line up for recess."

Charlotte immediately followed Miss Luna's directions and got behind her best friend, Madeline. They planned to play on the monkey bars. They loved swinging like monkeys!

The students burst through the hallway doors, as fast as a balloon losing its air. Eleven students were running in different directions. Some went straight for the slide, and others headed for the swings.

Most, like Charlotte and Madeline, were headed for the monkey bars.

Kevin was mean to Charlotte because she was smart. Instead of choosing to be kind, he made fun of her glasses. He thought he could pick on someone because they were different. Instead of choosing to be kind, he made fun of her. Kevin was a bully.

Charlotte used to be sensitive about her glasses and thought they made her eyes look really big. She hated being called names because glasses made her different.

One day, her mom told her that being different was what made her so awesome, kind, and smart!

Even though Miss Luna did not see Kevin's actions, Charlotte knew she had choices. She could let the boy's shove hurt her feelings, cry about being pushed down, or tattle on him. Instead, she chose to be kind and go for a walk.

Charlotte made the choice to be kind. She told Madeline she would be by the trees near the playground. Madeline waved and smiled in acknowledgment.

Charlotte was thinking about how much fun the kids were having on the monkey bars when all of a sudden, she heard the strangest sound.

It was faint at first, and she had to listen very carefully, but it sounded like crying or sniffling coming from above her head!

"Hello," Charlotte said again. This time she introduced herself, "My name is Charlotte, and I am a monkey too!"

"You're NOT a monkey," replied the voice in a defensive tone. He seemed sad and hurt. "You do NOT have a tail!"

"No, but I do love to swing and climb," Charlotte said, nodding her head enthusiastically.

"Yes," said the sad, blue monkey, still shaking his head, "but you are still NOT a monkey!"

"No, but bananas are my most favorite fruit in the world, and I love monkeying around! Don't you?" Charlotte asked with her big, blue eyes, sparkling as she looked up at the monkey.

"Yes," he replied, a little less upset now, "but you are still NOT a monkey! You do not live in the trees. We can NOT be friends."

"Of course we can be friends," said Charlotte with one hand on her hip. "I am just like you!"

"How?" asked the blue monkey, curiously.

"Well, I have a tree house, and you're in a tree. I am alone. You're alone, too. I seem to be different from my friends because I have glasses, but all I want to do is have fun, swing, and play games with those who are kind!"

The blue monkey could hardly believe his big, blue ears. "I am different too," he admitted. "You see, all of my friends are brown, as monkeys should be, but look at me!

I am BLUE!" With that, he jumped down at her feet, embarrassed!

Charlotte smiled warmly and said, "You are my favorite color. We will be best friends!"

The blue monkey, having never spoken to a human before, looked at this girl and noticed she was different.

She had two oval things on her face that made her eyes look even bigger and more blue! She WAS different too!

"But you are NOT a monkey," he stated again firmly. "We just cannot be friends!"

"It is true, I am NOT a monkey. I have no tail, I am not brown, and I live in a house," Charlotte said calmly, "but, I am thoughtful, kind, and love to play. Why can't I be your friend?"

The blue monkey was stumped and shrugged his blue shoulders. Charlotte continued, "We also both love climbing and swinging. What else could matter?" The monkey could not respond.

"Of course," replied Charlotte, "see you later!" and with that she ran back to the school and waved with a smile on her face.

The rest of the school day went by quickly. In art class, Charlotte made her new friend a multi-shaded, blue friendship bracelet. She wanted them to be friends forever!

Charlotte kept blue monkey her secret, and she got an extra banana for him at lunch.

Luckily, she lived near the school and was old enough to walk home. She packed up the bananas and got in the walker's line, holding on tightly to the friendship bracelet.

"Hi!" she called with excitement. "I cannot stay long, Mommy will be waiting for me at home, but I have a few minutes to play. I made this friendship bracelet for you!"

She handed him the blue, braided bracelet. The blue monkey had a huge smile on his face as he took her gift.

When they finished their bananas, Charlotte's swinging lessons began. The first few times were hard, and she fell. He helped her up and chose to be kind and give her an encouraging hug and smile.

While both Charlotte and the blue monkey learned a great deal from one another that afternoon, the most important lesson they learned was that looks and DIFFERENCES DO NOT MATTER AT ALL, WHEN IT COMES TO FRIENDSHIP! Kindness and an open heart are all that truly matter!

Charlotte asked, "What is your name?"

Now proud of his color, he said, "You may call me, 'Blue Monkey!'"

Just as Charlotte learned to accept her glasses, he too, accepted his color as part of what made him awesome.

The two hugged and went their separate ways for the afternoon with plans to play again tomorrow.

Remember YOU too have a choice to be kind. Kindness makes others feel accepted and may help you make new friends as well!

The End